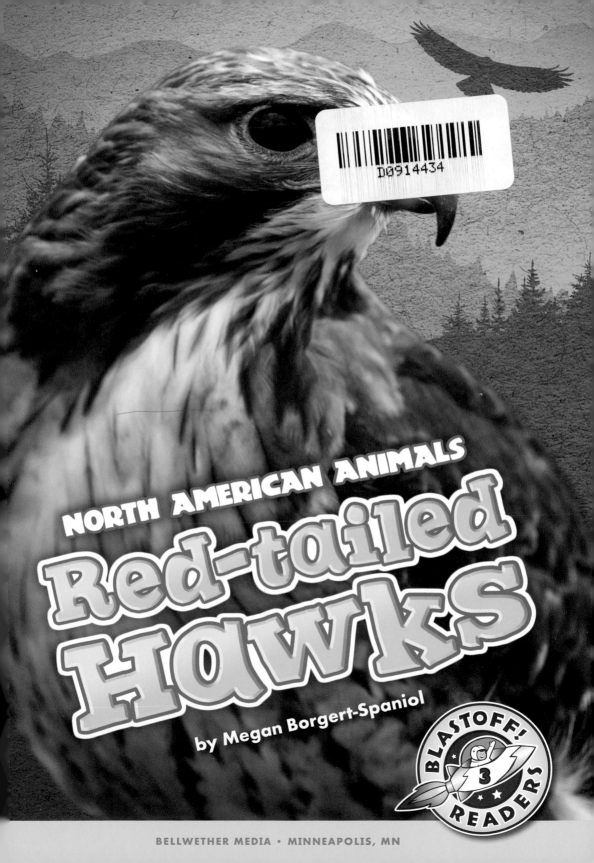

NORTH AMERICAN ANIMALS

Red-tailed Hawks

by Megan Borgert-Spaniol

BLASTOFF! 3 READERS

BELLWETHER MEDIA • MINNEAPOLIS, MN

Note to Librarians, Teachers, and Parents:

Blastoff! Readers are carefully developed by literacy experts and combine standards-based content with developmentally appropriate text.

Level 1 provides the most support through repetition of high-frequency words, light text, predictable sentence patterns, and strong visual support.

Level 2 offers early readers a bit more challenge through varied simple sentences, increased text load, and less repetition of high-frequency words.

Level 3 advances early-fluent readers toward fluency through increased text and concept load, less reliance on visuals, longer sentences, and more literary language.

Level 4 builds reading stamina by providing more text per page, increased use of punctuation, greater variation in sentence patterns, and increasingly challenging vocabulary.

Level 5 encourages children to move from "learning to read" to "reading to learn" by providing even more text, varied writing styles, and less familiar topics.

Whichever book is right for your reader, Blastoff! Readers are the perfect books to build confidence and encourage a love of reading that will last a lifetime!

This edition first published in 2015 by Bellwether Media, Inc.

No part of this publication may be reproduced in whole or in part without written permission of the publisher. For information regarding permission, write to Bellwether Media, Inc., Attention: Permissions Department, 5357 Penn Avenue South, Minneapolis, MN 55419.

Library of Congress Cataloging-in-Publication Data

Borgert-Spaniol, Megan, 1989-
  Red-tailed Hawks / by Megan Borgert-Spaniol.
    pages cm. – (Blastoff! Readers. North American Animals)
  Includes bibliographical references and index.
  Summary: "Simple text and full-color photography introduce beginning readers to red-tailed hawks. Developed by literacy experts for students in kindergarten through third grade"– Provided by publisher.
  ISBN 978-1-62617-194-7 (hardcover : alk. paper)
  1. Red-tailed hawk–Juvenile literature. I. Title.
  QL696.F32B66 2015
  598.9'44–dc23
                                                    2014037315

Printed in the United States of America, North Mankato, MN.

Table of Contents

What Are Red-tailed Hawks?

Red-tailed hawks are **raptors**. They are the most common hawks in North America.

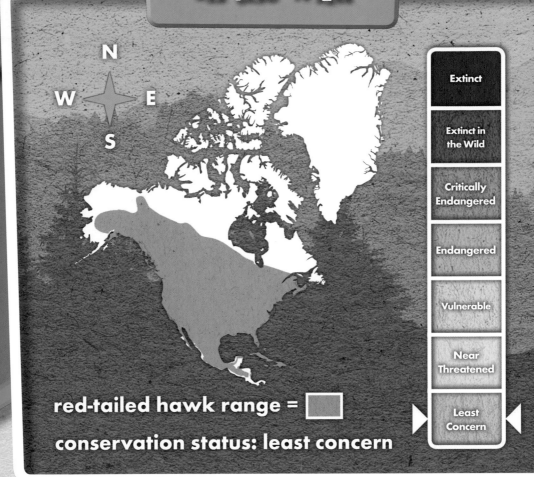

In the Wild

N
W — E
S

Extinct

Extinct in the Wild

Critically Endangered

Endangered

Vulnerable

Near Threatened

Least Concern

red-tailed hawk range = ▢

conservation status: least concern

These birds make their homes in grasslands, deserts, **scrublands**, and woodlands. They can also be spotted over farm fields and city parks.

Identify a Red-tailed Hawk

rusty
red tail

rounded
wings

hooked
beak

Red-tailed hawks are named for their rusty red tails. Most have brown bodies with light bellies.

Some in the west are dark or reddish brown all over.

Birds of Prey

Red-tailed hawks are **carnivores**. They hunt for mice, voles, rabbits, and squirrels. They also feed on snakes, birds, and **carrion**.

deer mice

meadow voles

cottontail rabbits

gray squirrels

western diamondback
rattlesnakes

ring-necked
pheasants

Red-tailed hawks watch the ground from tall trees, telephone poles, and other high **perches**.

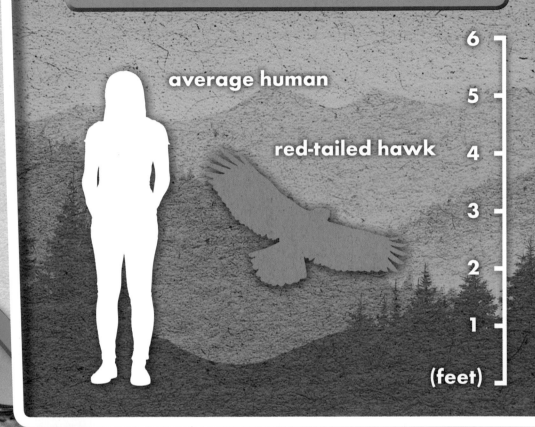

Size of a Red-tailed Hawk

average human

red-tailed hawk

6
5
4
3
2
1
(feet)

They also soar in circles. A red-tailed hawk's wings measure about 4 feet (1.2 meters) when spread out.

A red-tailed hawk
dives to attack **prey**.

It grabs its meal with strong **talons** and a sharp beak.

Food can be hard to find in cold, snowy areas.

Red-tailed hawks in the north often **migrate** south for winter.

Nests, Eggs, and Chicks

A male and female work together to build a nest on a tree branch or cliff ledge.

The nest is made of twigs, bark, and pine needles. It can be 3 feet (1 meter) wide.

The female lays one to five eggs in the nest. She and the male take turns keeping the eggs warm. **Chicks** hatch after four to five weeks.

Name for babies:	chicks
Number of eggs laid:	1 to 5 eggs
Time spent inside egg:	4 to 5 weeks
Time spent with parents:	about 3 months

Newborn chicks are covered in white **down**. Darker feathers grow in over the next several weeks.

Young red-tailed hawks become **fledglings** at six to seven weeks. Then their parents teach them to fly and hunt. Soon they are ready to soar on their own!

Glossary

carnivores—animals that only eat meat

carrion—the rotting meat of a dead animal

chicks—baby red-tailed hawks

down—soft feathers that keep birds warm

fledglings—young birds that have feathers for flight

migrate—to travel from one place to another, often with the seasons

newborn—just recently born

perches—high places from which red-tailed hawks can watch for prey

prey—animals that are hunted by other animals for food

raptors—large birds that hunt other animals; raptors have excellent eyesight and powerful talons.

scrublands—dry lands with short bushes and trees

talons—the strong, sharp claws of red-tailed hawks and other raptors

To Learn More

AT THE LIBRARY

Alderfer, Jonathan K. *National Geographic Kids Bird Guide of North America: The Best Birding Book for Kids from National Geographic's Bird Experts.* Washington, D.C.: National Geographic, 2013.

Sill, Cathryn P. *About Raptors.* Atlanta, Ga.: Peachtree Publishers, 2010.

Vail, Grace. *Hunting with Hawks.* New York, N.Y.: Gareth Stevens Publishing, 2014.

ON THE WEB

Learning more about red-tailed hawks is as easy as 1, 2, 3.

1. Go to www.factsurfer.com.

2. Enter "red-tailed hawks" into the search box.

3. Click the "Surf" button and you will see a list of related web sites.

With factsurfer.com, finding more information is just a click away.

Index

The images in this book are reproduced through the courtesy of: LesPalenik, front cover; Tania Thomson, pp. 4-5; Chris Hill, p. 6 (top left); Dawn Wilson Photo, p. 6 (top center); Robert Eastman, p. 6 (top right); Paul Reeves Photography, p. 6 (bottom); Tony Campbell, p. 7; Sanjibbhatt, pp. 8-9; Close Encounters Photo, p. 9 (top left); Magnus Manske/ Wikipedia, p. 9 (top right); Michael Chatt, p. 9 (center left); IrinaK, p. 9 (center right); Audrey Snider-Bell, p. 9 (bottom left); Tom Reichner, p. 9 (bottom right); CHKnox, pp. 10-11; JIM ZIPP/ Getty Images, p. 12; Ray Whitt/ Corbis, pp. 12-13; Wayne Lynch/ Glow Images, p. 14; Wild Nature Photos/ Animals Animals, pp. 16-17; Robbie George/ Getty Images, pp. 18-19; Joesboy, p. 19; Ryan Houston/ Getty Images, pp. 20-21.